Red Tape
Your
Night Light

Smoke ~~Drink~~ Draw

park

park

THERES POISON IN THE WATER
AND THEY ARE BURNING
ALL THE BOOKS
Grapevine rumors
CAUSED THE DIRTY LOOKS
Self Esteem CUM CLEAN
WOULD RATHER BE IN UR
WET DREAM ..... AH HH
YEAH HAHA ~~LOST OF THEM~~
~~THE WAY~~ I WOULD.
REALLY THO ... AHH
⊙ LOST MY THOUGHT STREAM
   ...
   Dont think I can
      redeem
   THIS ONE for the team.
   Good bye Sun beam

Penny bought all her course books at the university bookstore
she waited in lines for identification cards, dining hall passes,
Reading alcohol policies and std stats

Weeks passed
She did assignments without caring

School was easy, obvious, questions asked over and over.
she knew the answers. She forgot everything. surviving on short-term
memory
Penny smoked a cigarette in the sun on the stone steps of grand buildings
she chatted with a little birdie, whispering,
"we didn't have to go to college to learn great things"

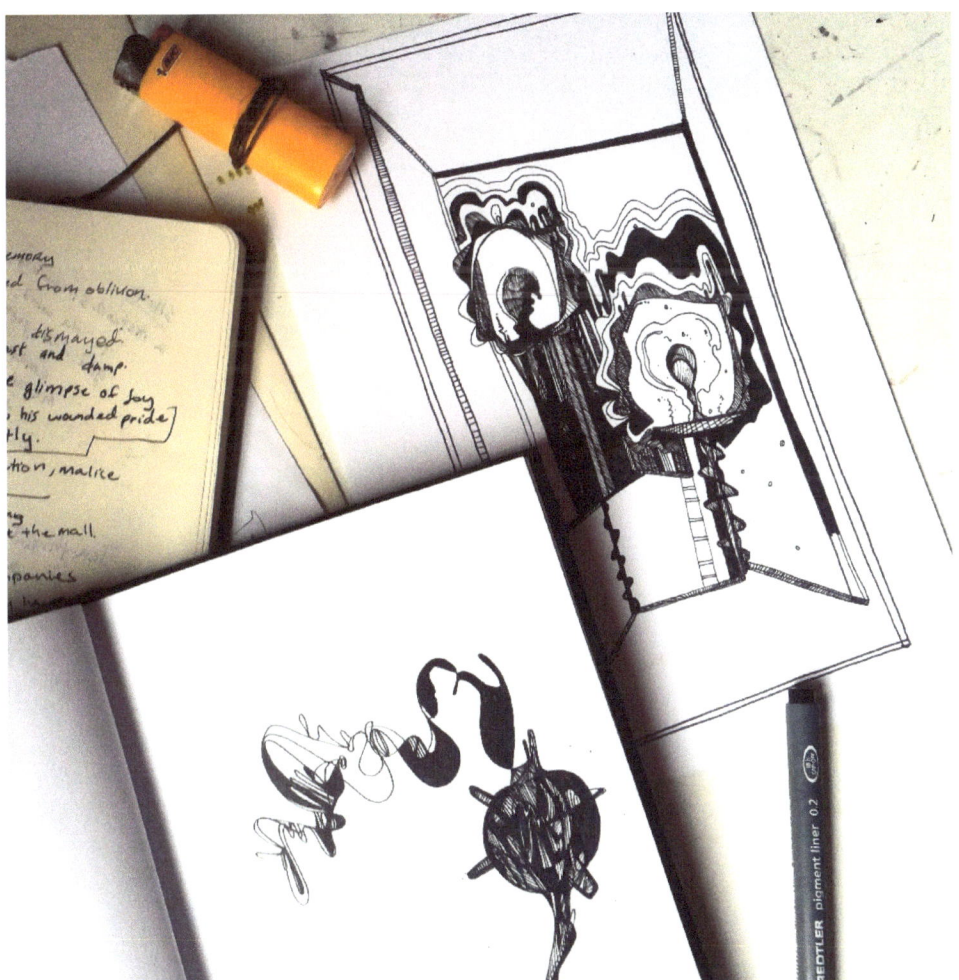

Peter was tired of applying himself.

Peter was tired of applying himself
Tired of pumping out papers about things
He didn't really care about
School buildings were lifeless

The higher the education
The higher the price tag

He was most bored when in a classroom
The 4 walls
The stale air
The drone of his professor's voice
Peter needed someone to respect

Bird shit dries on a statue of someone significant
Students walked across campus with coffee
with cigarette
with damp hair
with campus food prepared
Teachers didn't inspire Peter,
He had moments when he believed everyone to be lazy morons
He showed violent tendencies
He had trouble sleeping
And being alone
People cluster to destroy themselves.
Peter melted into the mess.
They destroyed things. They didn't care.
He didn't think his friends were bad.

Just unsatisfied.

It was 11pm on a Friday night. Campus was littered with college drunks. Penny dumped the contains of her red solo cup into some bushes by a frat house. Alcohol took the shyness away but she couldn't help wondering if there were better worlds than this, better thoughts to be thinking. The faint smell of marijuana caught her attention and she took it as a sign. She cut across the dark dewy field towards a cluster of apartments.

Inside the first floor apartment, Peter filled the bong with better thoughts and handed it to her. He watched her clear the smoke knowing she would be gone before day break;
she was always gone before day break.
Penny filled the bong with other worlds and handed it to him. She watched him clear the smoke finally understanding why dawn was called mourning.

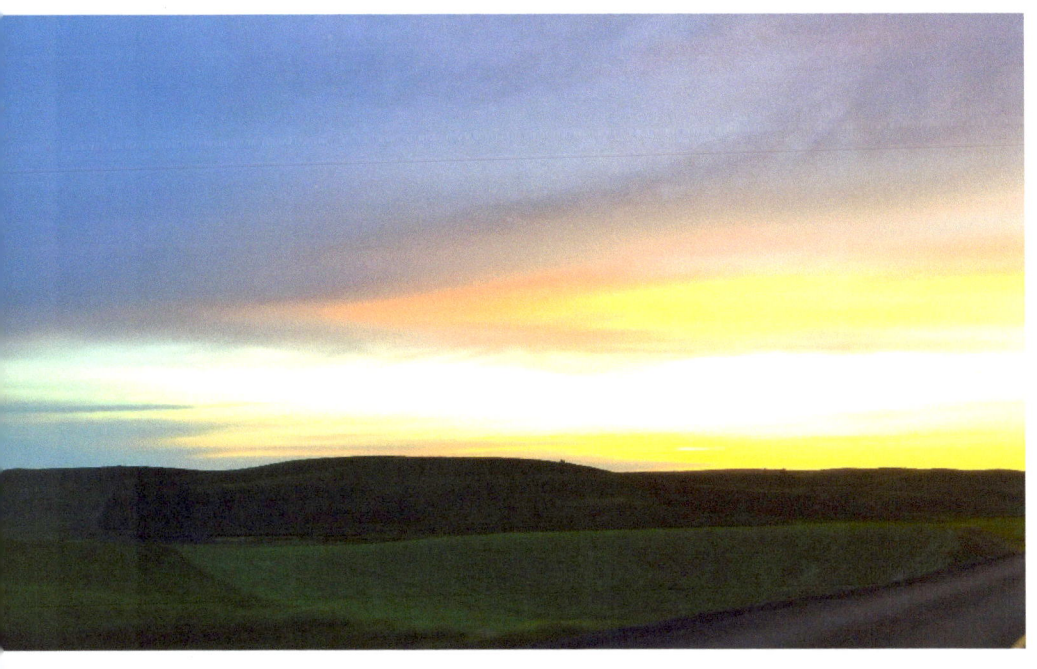

the
dilation
of
pupils.

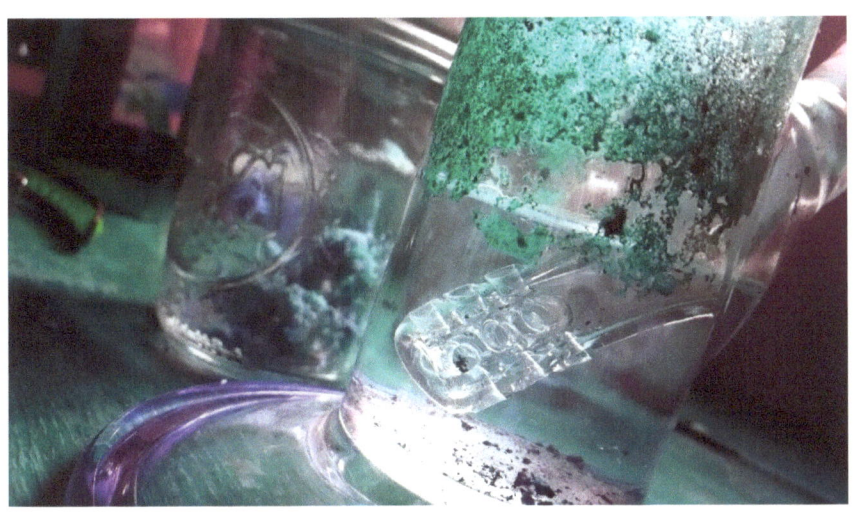

Slow motion tangle
Half my mind is aware and the other half is
Lost
The time of day is a blurrrr and so are my thoughts
Aimless wander
Got me asking where you been ?
When will I see you again ?
Hey, you got
Time to spend? With me?
Because the heart muscle is an interesting thing
It hasn't always been my brain's best friend
It's a meshy
Messy blend
Hard to comprehend when she's playin
Pretend

Slow motion tangle
Coming at the right angle
Half my mind is unaware
of the loveliest death
Strangle.

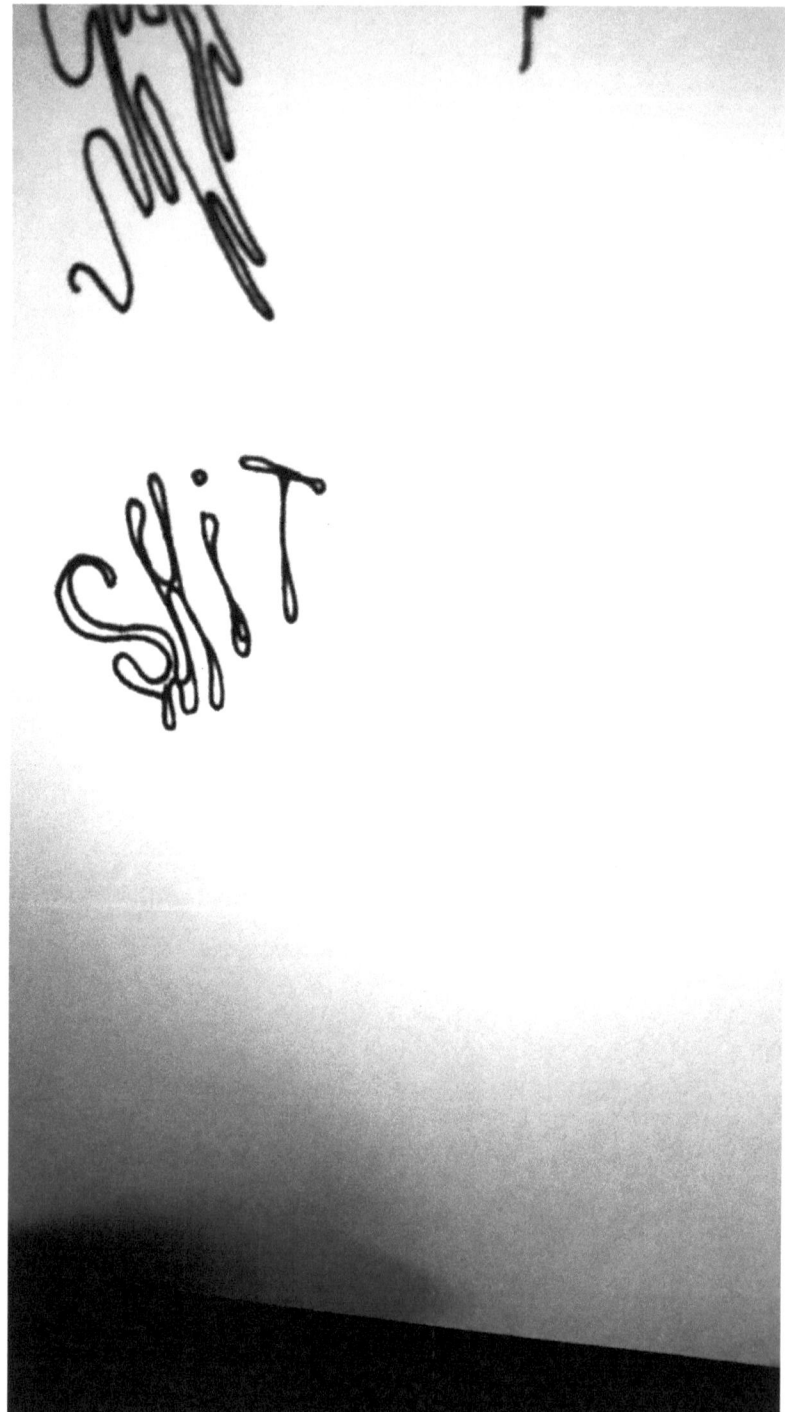

The alcoholic slumber and a hangover to feed.
Smoked all the dope. Forgot why your head hurt

You   don't   laugh   as   much   as   you   used   to
But you don't cry as much either

You wanna love in the morning
You wanna get thru the day
You might eat if you can keep it down
You might drink if you can black out
you might run around run around if you can afford some bad decisions
you might taste like cigarettes and alcohol, screaming things like,
Hey, thanks for nothing at all.

If you can find the right intoxicants........ ....

they   say,   the   difference   between   a   drug
and
a poison
is the dosage.

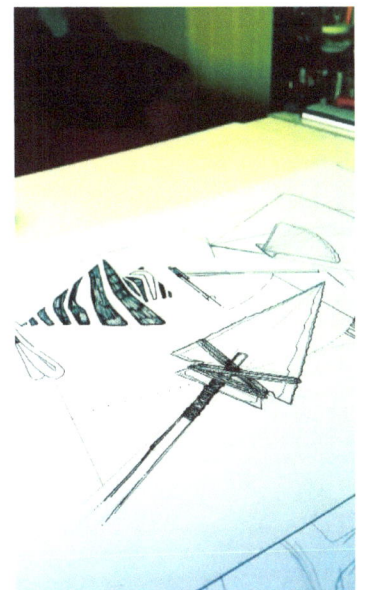

Penny went on a roadtrip she believed would go on forever…

'I'm in this awful place called bum fuck, ' she cried into the pay phone.

Peter asked, 'Where are you?'

He couldn't hear her.
 He was standing outside a gray mall in Idaho handing out flyers to gray looking Americans.

'In this awful place called bum fuck, if you have a map I'll help you locate it,'

' I don't have a map at the moment, Penny, I'm sort of busy,'

'Sort of busy doing what?'
'Educating the masses,'

Each piece of paper Peter handed out said life guarantees nothing, but people just thought they were getting coupons for the food court.

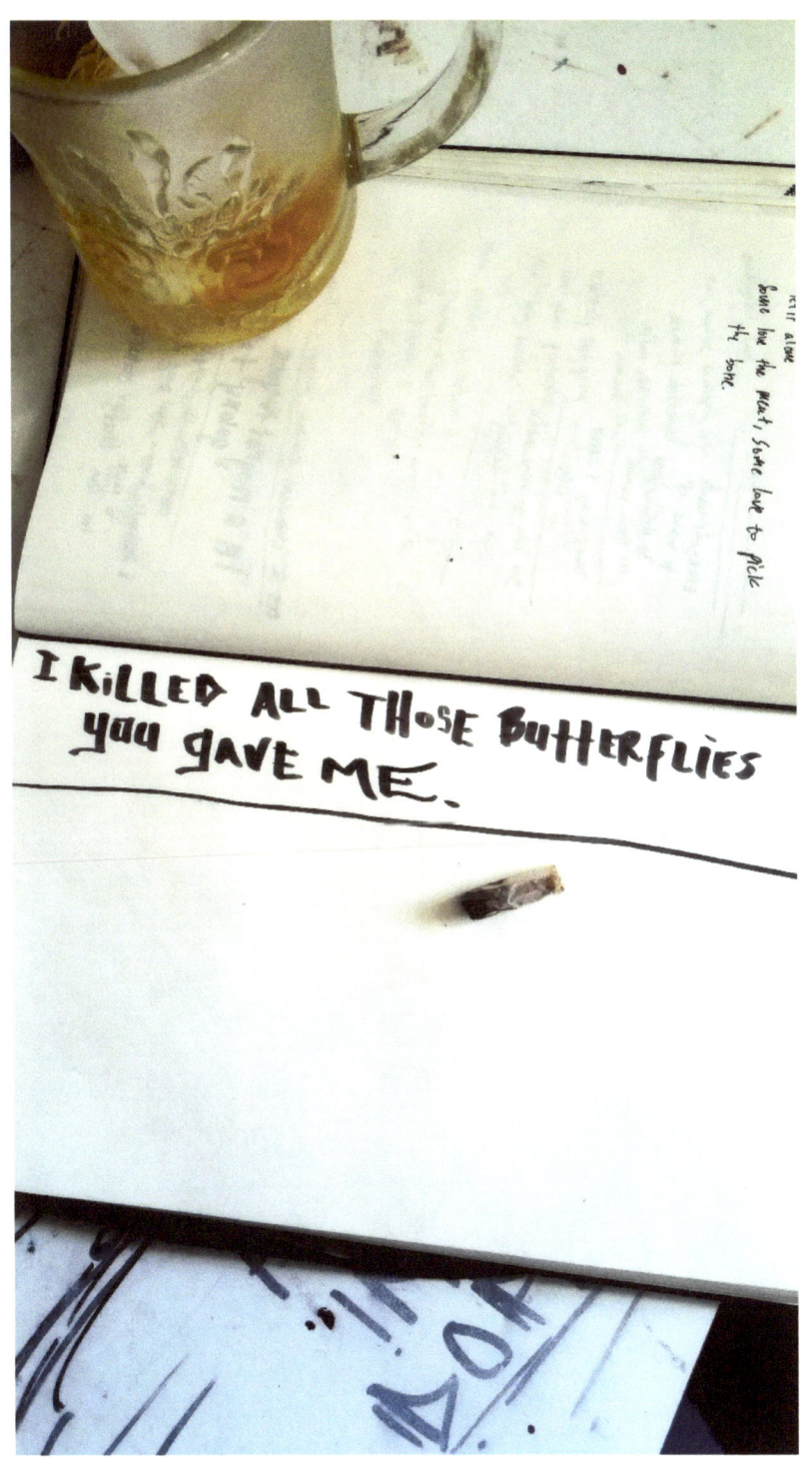

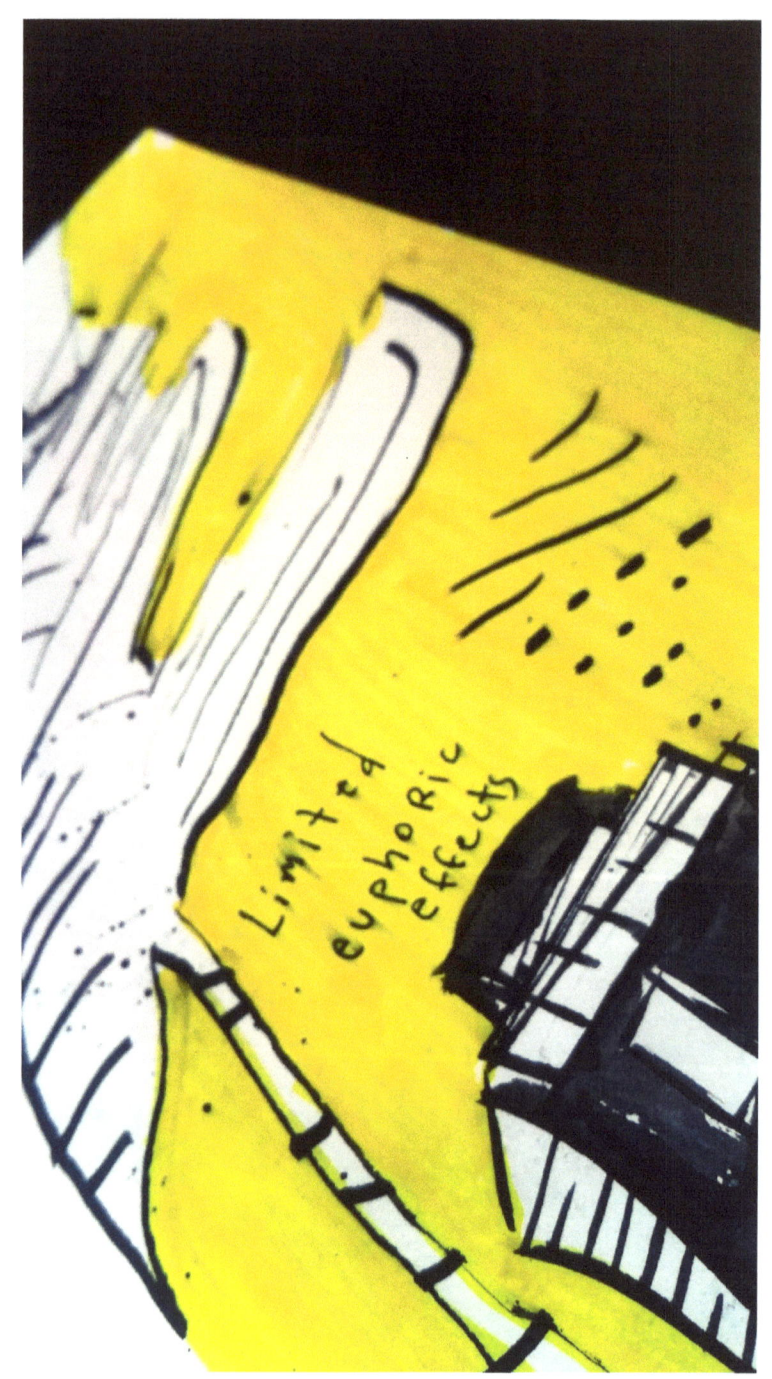

She doesn't get up early

It takes a long time to exist
She comes to life in the moonlight
She connects
All the dots on my skin
Up my arm her ink drips drops across my collar bone
Fleshy tentacles wrapping around my neck
Stabbing my eye
Invading my mind
Damn brilliant camouflaged in the sky
Am I too light sensitive
To ask why?

Straw in her pbr

Tequila shocker poppers on my porch
During dead week

Cheers on cheers down the street
Side by side
I drunk lean on you
You drunk lean on me
Its greeeen
So very grassssy green
The baseline to my primetime
Its greeeen so very grassy greeeen
She says, fuck me be you.
Need it, want it, crave it

Mad.
Mad over the moon.
Mad about you
Touch my face
Can you feel the drunk?

"You can sterilize all you want, its still dirt."

Can we be at peace even with these dissatisfactions?

We are what we are.

Peter and Penny, twisted energy
Posted on September 8, 2013

They ran chaotic paths.
Colliding into each other.
Fusing and melting.

Then scattering again.
A cycle of undocumented energy.

Peter and Penny tasted a freedom that none of us would ever know.

they bonded over bad habits,

of chemicals,

of alcohol,

they experiment with minds

with reality,

with perception,

The slope got slippery

and they started to fall,

into the rabbit hole

the two would crawl,

side by side,

with curious eyes and excited souls,

into the center of the world,

the

two

would

go.

Penny snapped, 'but your mind stops working when you're dead,'
Posted on August 26, 2013

Peter was in the living room, painting the walls egg shell white.

12dollars an hour sounded pretty good at the time…

4hours later his head was heavy from the fumes.

"Peter," Penny barked. She hung in the door way, impatiently waiting.

He was only half listening to her, 'I dont know Penny…Heaven is probably…. just whatever you make it… in your mind,'

She didnt understand why he wasnt more concerned.

Penny snapped, 'but your mind stops working when you're dead,'

He shrugged, 'better figure it out now, I guess'

And dipped his brush into a can of paint. Rolling and spreading thick globs of white paint. Repeating the process over and over again.

Mundanely creating more mundane

Penny rolled her eyes, "Death better not be like a room of egg shell white"

Peter thought, I can't wait

His father told him,

only rich people go to therapy,

because poor people have shit to do.

And Peter thought,

I cant wait to go to therapy…

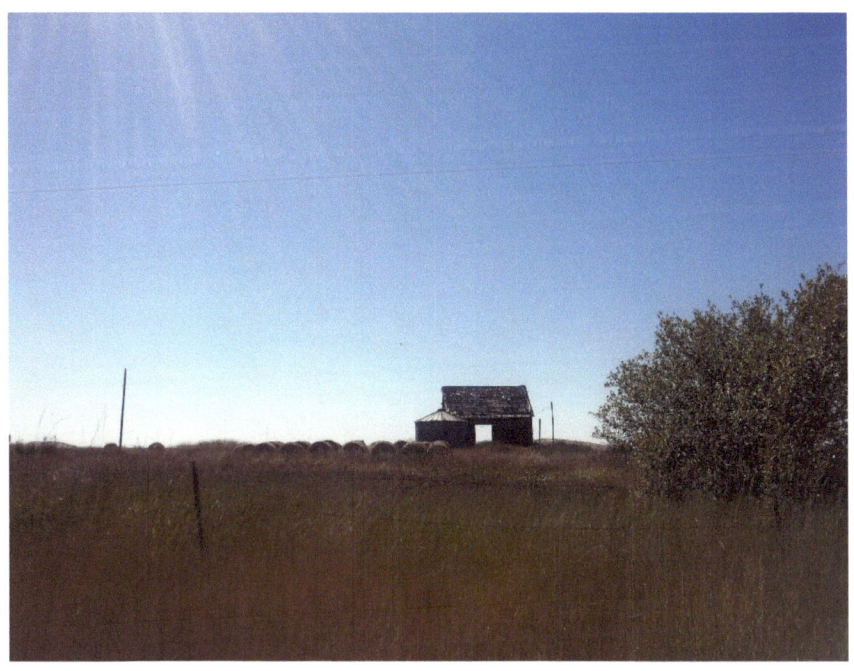

Slowly realizing his friends were professional drunks

Peter looked out of place. He drank each beer with a face of heavy thought.

Intelligent minds were now boozed soaked brains.

His friends weren't that different from himself, they just wanted to feel normal. Someone bought a round of shots and Peter started doing simple multiplication problems in his head,

trying to determine how drunk

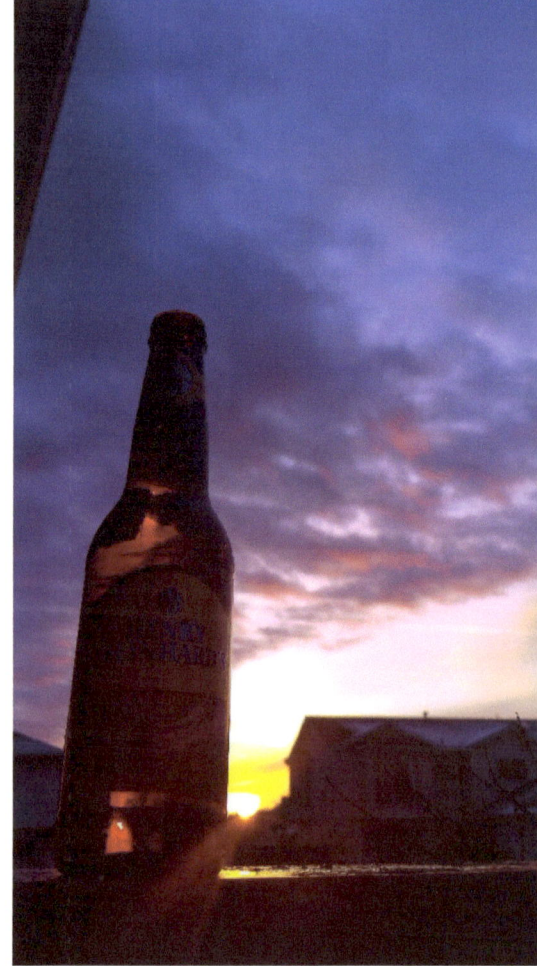

he really was.

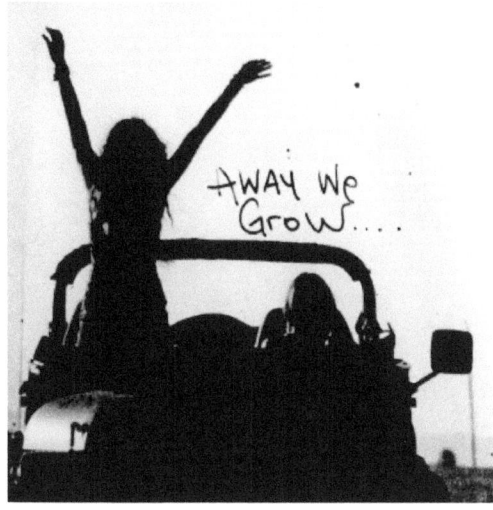

Two summers have passed since the last time Peter was in her presence. His stomach twisted. Nerves and hunger.

When he arrived at an expensive cabin, a stillness touched his pulse. He slipped thru the open front door and found her in the kitchen.
Sitting on the counter swinging her feet.
Sun-bleached hair, in a sun-bleached dress,
she confessed, 'drugs make me feel like I have super powers,'
Peter leaned in the door way, he spoke slowly, 'remember that you're not jesus christ,'
Her eyes smiled. His gut moaned. Hunger. Nerves. He reached for a muffin but stopped. Her hand was warm on top of his.
'don't eat that,' she said hopping down, 'there's all sorts of lsd'
He examined the muffin with debating eyes and went to fridge. No water bottles or beer, but there were six bottles of orange juice.
He picked one up suspiciously.
'Don't eat or drink anything in this house,' she warned walking by him, smelling of wildflowers she winked, 'there are drugs in everything,'
A flower was tangling in her hair. he gently rescued it asking, 'how many people live here Penny?'
'I'm not really sure. But we should go to town. So we can get clean food,'

Her pupils were dilated. Peter wasn't sure if it was because of him or because of the muffins.

She skipped out the door and towards his truck slowly twirling a white daisy, lacing it between her fingers.

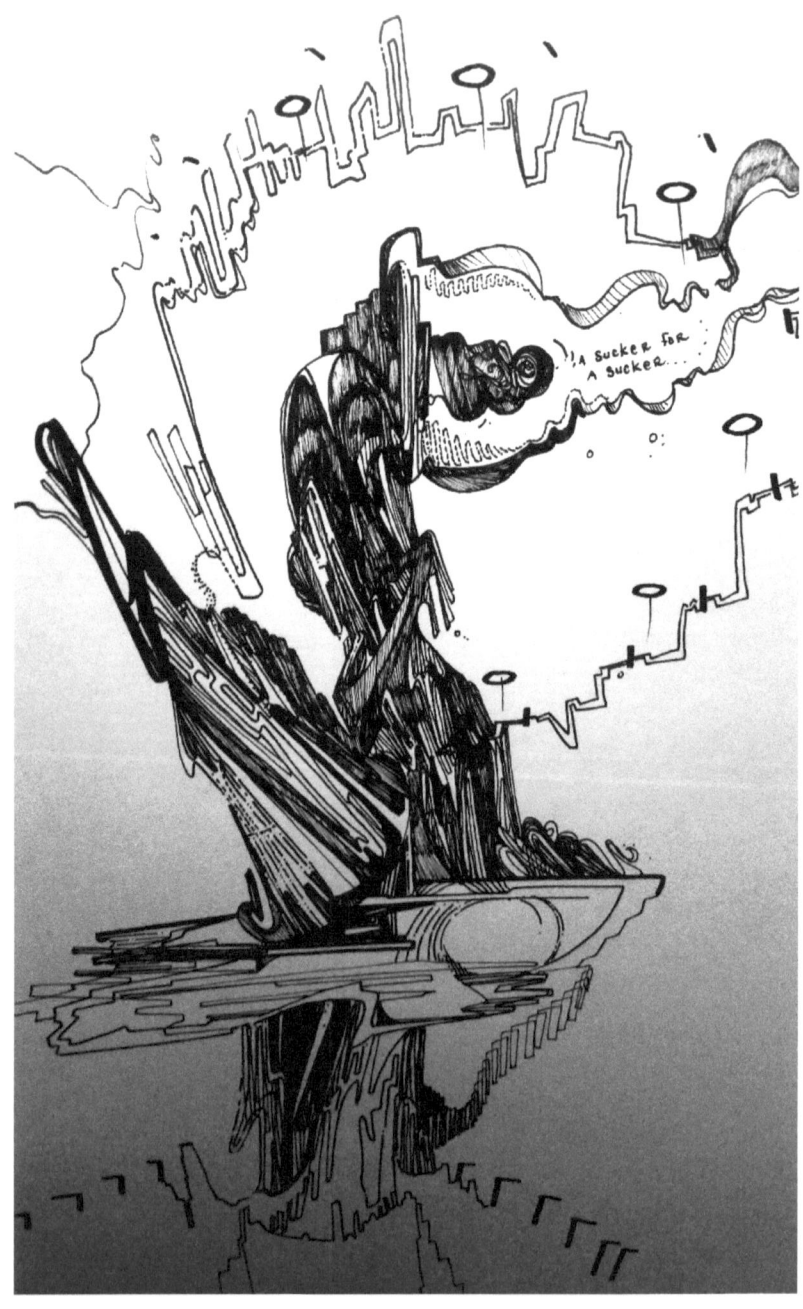

penny groaned, just kill me
Posted on February 1, 2014

She groaned, 'just kill me already,'

Peter had just walk thru the door with car keys and a small bag of weed in hand.
'just… kill me…just end it,'
. Blankets were covering all the windows. All the lights were turned off except for a small spinning disco ball in the center of the living room. Bits of white reflected light danced around the living room.

Penny sighed, 'just do it, just kill me, what's the point anymore?'
Peter set his keys on the table and closed the door behind him.
It took him a moment to recognize the table had been moved. He picked his keys off the floor realizing the couch has been moved too, and the desk, the loveseat, coffee table. Some of the artwork had been removed, even the neon green cat statue wasn't where he left it. Or was it? The house was so dark…the disco ball just kept spinning… sprinkling scraps of light around the room… like pieces of confetti.

What happened here? How long had he been gone?

'Penny penny penny' Peter mutters fumbling around in the dark. What kind of madness was created in here? He found a chair covered in feathers…or was it silly string? he brushed it off and sat next to a fish tank he had never seen before.

Where did this come from? Where are the fish?
Turning the aquarium light on he finally spotted Penny in the corner, sprawled out on a bean bag buried under blankets and books. Funny kind of creature.

'just kill me already,' she whined again.
'oh I don't wanna hear it, penny, not again,'

'I mean it peter, just do it,' she groaned later, 'just kill me,'
'I'm not gonna do it but… why?'

'because whats the point? What's the point of living? Life will never be as grand as these novels. Look at them, they are wonderful. The pages and print, the beautiful well-crafted poetic stories. With thought provoking ideas! and then... look at this life, all phony and fuck,'

All phony and fuck, Peter chuckled rocking the freshly rolled joint between his fingers.

All phony and fuck.
He lit the end of it and inhaled, 'well maybe your phony fuck life will become a grand novel, do you really want me to kill you in the middle of it?'
She sat up, books and blankets falling to the floor, 'how do you know you would be killing me in the middle and not at the end?'

He exhaled, 'If I kill you at the end that makes me the bad guy, and I'm not the bad guy,'
'Fine, so kill me in the middle, whatever,'
'I cant do that either,'

'why not?' she snapped.

Peter shook his head and let the high rush in and he shrugged and stated,
'Main characters aren't killed in the middle, Penny...Besides what would I do?...you know...for the rest of the story...without... you?'

'murder suicide'

Peter shook his head again, 'Penny,'
'what?'

'you wanna come over here and smoke some of this with me?'
'not really,'

'i think you should, please, you are freaking me out a lil bit,'
'ok... but you come to me,'

. . .

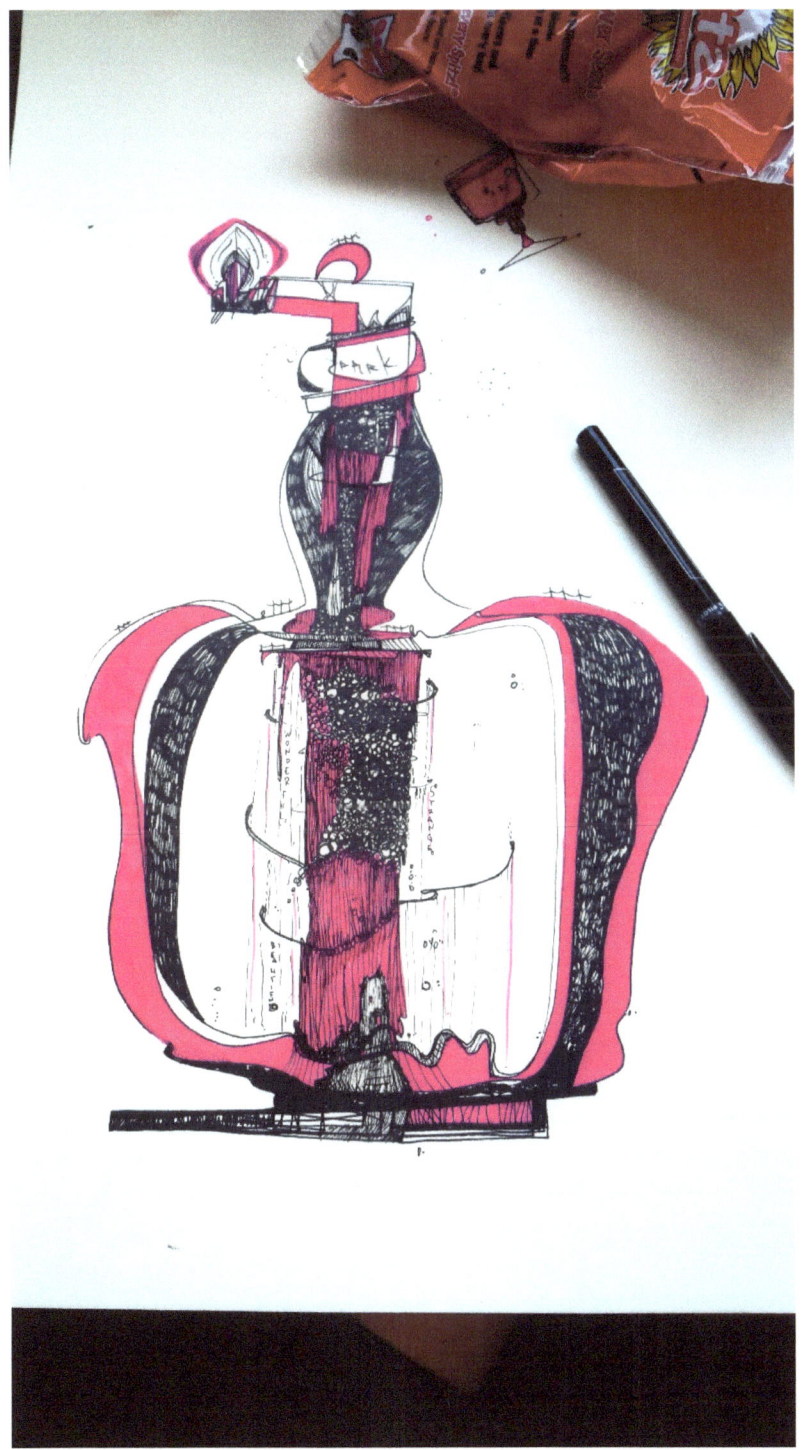

Peter&Penny.

A jolly mess. An escapist. Youthfully. Reckless.

late one night
Scratched down into his notebook
He wrote:

After a party, penny looked extremely fucked up, she motioned me to follow her into the bathroom. And I shit you not, penny coughed out a tiny purple seahorse into the sink.

It was the most memorizing thing my eyes have ever seen

This tiny water creature wiggled in perfect harmony

Penny laughed
Saying, excuse me, how surreal was that? Third time this week. Then she flushed the happy seahorse away, down the forever drain.

They wouldn't see each other again until years later

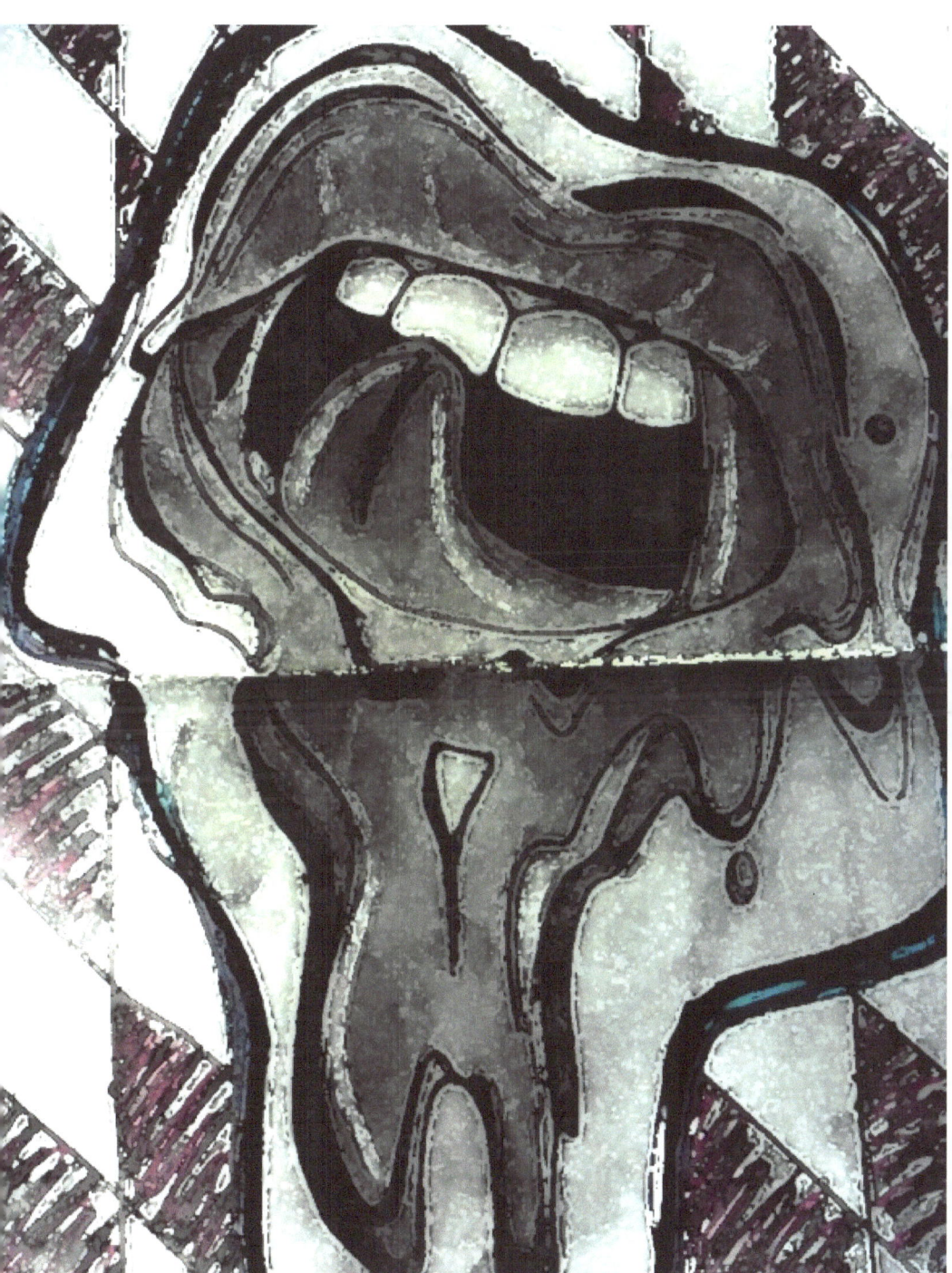

Mind and muscle seize

I just stare
Catatonic
Teeth don't sit right in my jaw
Im convinced they shift in my sleep

Tiresome confusion
Squeezes my brain tissue
Inside my skull

Too much light burns
My eyes
Igniting all this

Electrical activity

Curiosity

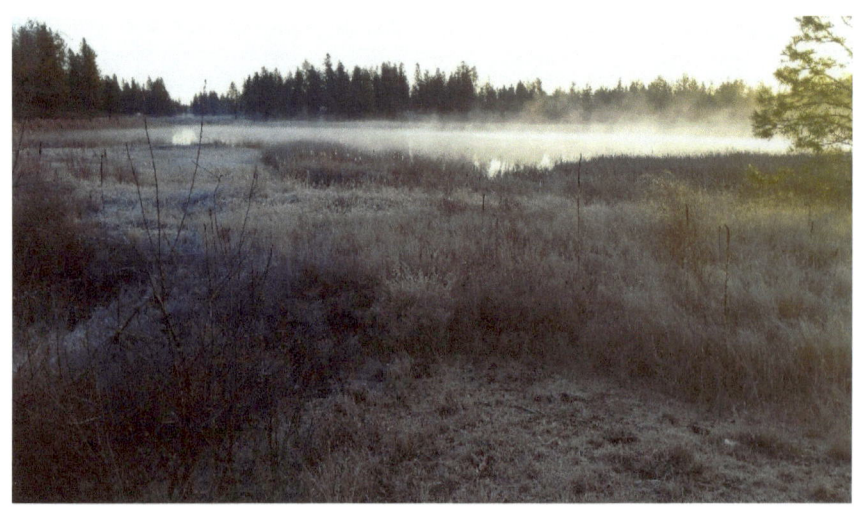

<u>a damn near fatal performance</u>
Posted on April 3, 2014 edited September 2, 2015

at first it appears necessary
c o n form ing   felt
ordinary and like new prospects then she appears

then she appears in a red dress to address the group as a whole

her smile her look

a flattering performance damn near flawless, a bisexual temptress she
appears she appears in a red dress
from a cloud of smoke in her presence
warmly received she is buzzingly bright light considering her morally
questionable appearance. doesnt apologize for using profanity, no fake
concern for respectability she'll whisper sexy lies in your ears sugar-coating
x-rated promises
at first it appears necessary conforming felt ordinary new prospects
filled their heads then she appears in a red dress from a cloud of smoke in
her presence

are you alive or are you dead
are you alive or are you dead selling emotions for profit she'll fill your
head selling emotions for profit

are you alive? or are you dead?
she appears in a red dress smoke upon her lips, gun on her hip slips, springs and clips
    a deadly temptress
    a damn near fatal performance
    at first it appears necessary
    a deadly temptress
    a damn near fatal performance.

The most beautiful thing about her...

The most beautiful thing about her wasn't her soul, it was her mouth. And if I'm gonna be really honest it wasn't really **what** she was saying that attracted *me* to *her*, but the **way** that she said it. Her voice rang a silver bell inside my cage of ribs that I didn't even know existed.

A surreal surprise. A resonating sensation. Enlightenment. Nirvana. **Kurt Cobain.**

When she spoke.

Warm nectar drops of sound traveled down my ear canal. Liquid gold puddled up against my ear drum. It's one of those things that's so good it shouldn't occur, in this life time or the next because we aren't worthy. Words passing thru her lips just became sweeter. Sweeter in sound. Sweeter in taste.

I'd bet my cat's ninth life on that statement. I was jonsing. Jonsing hard for my words to pass thru her sexy mouthpart. I needed them to escape from her tight voice box, shimmy up her long and lovely vocal cords, loop around her pink tongue, slip passed her lips, and penetrate my audio cortex. AND ring. Ring! RING! that silver bell inside my empty vessel of a being.

Ring it. Again and again.

Because. this.
Is the kind of stimulation
I have been craving.

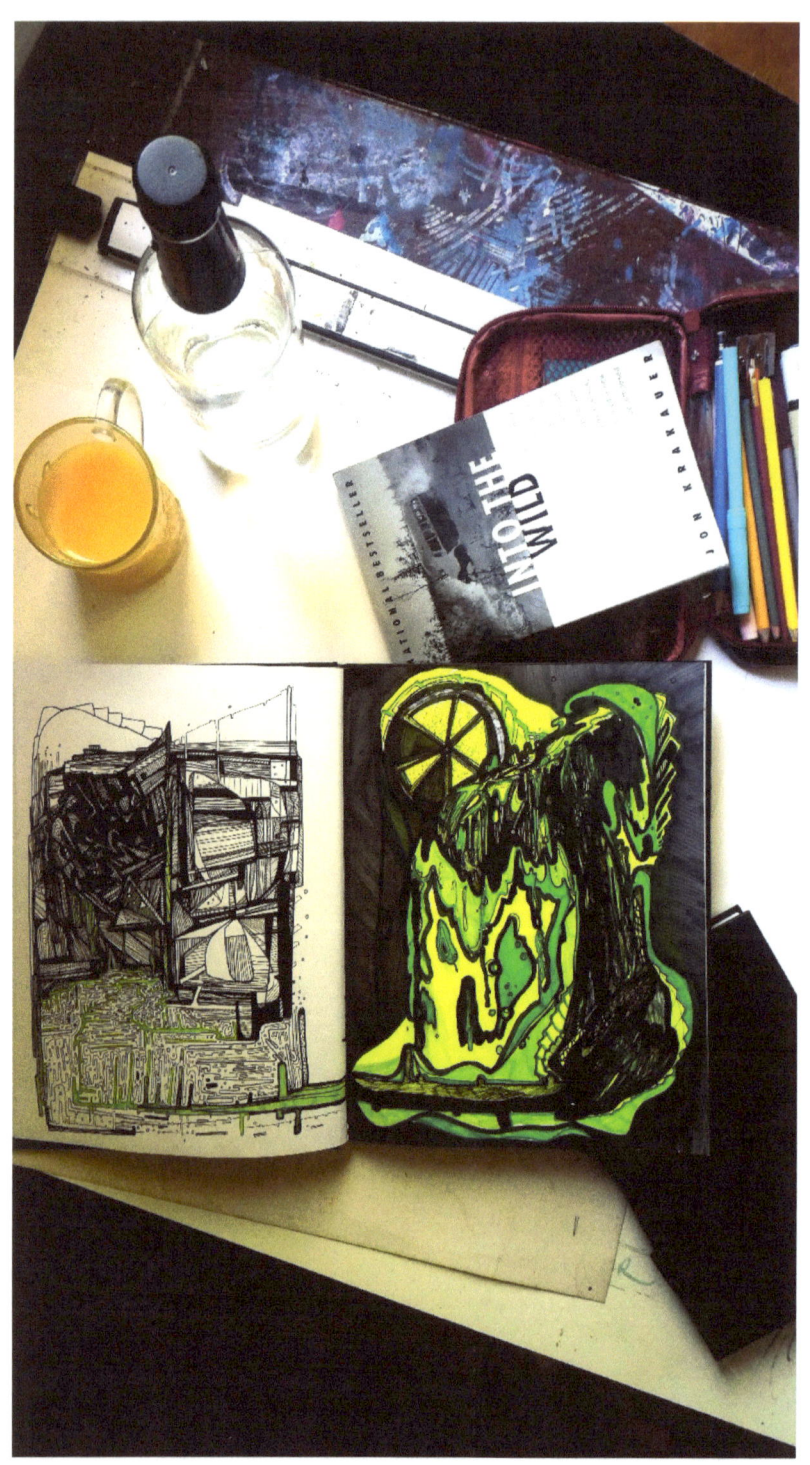

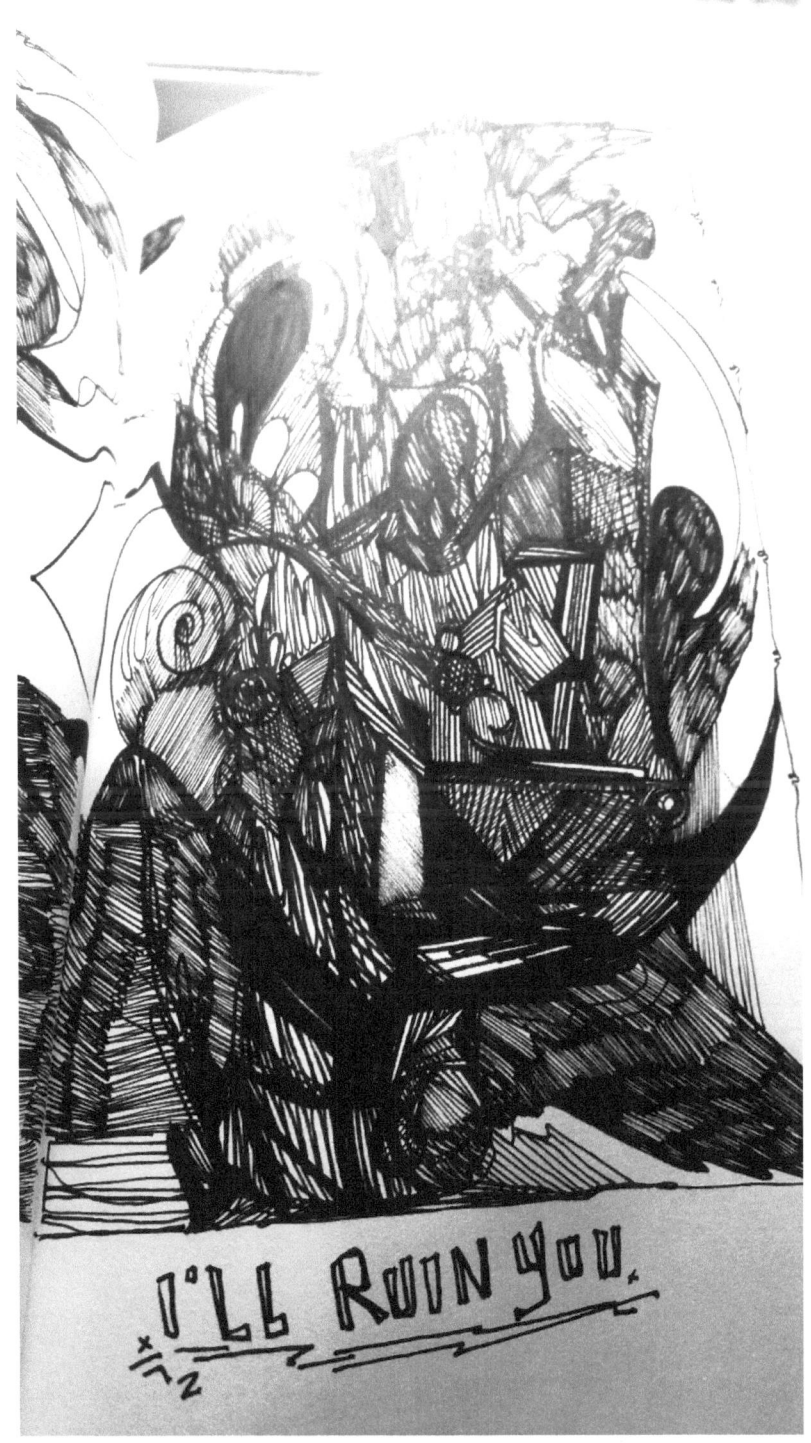

WORLD'S CLASSIEST TRUCK STOP

Road trippin
Oxy cotton
Fluffy Floating
We were joking
Peroxide sterilized
We were high
Concrete flying
Powerline riding
Would you walk
With me?
Thru the pollution industry?
I'll buy a bottle
Of the finest
Gasoline
Share pulls under the dead tree
Wonder why the river isn't clean
Just evidence of business booming
Picking money off of plants
Consuming
Oxy cotton
Fluffy Floating
We were choking on clouds
We were joking on smog

High flying low riding thru the pollution industry

Well worn whatever

Clothing cutting cuties cause
Fetish
Mind eraser
This drunk tongue wrestles another
Touching inappropriate under the table
Locked in
Locked in love's loveseat
Well worn whatever
Naked for the warm weather
Green beer bottles all over the table
A drunk tongue wrestles another
Pin up girl
Diva diving in public displays of affection
Touching touching touching
Inappropriate
Under the table
Clothing cutting cuties
Cause fetish
Naked
Nice
Weather

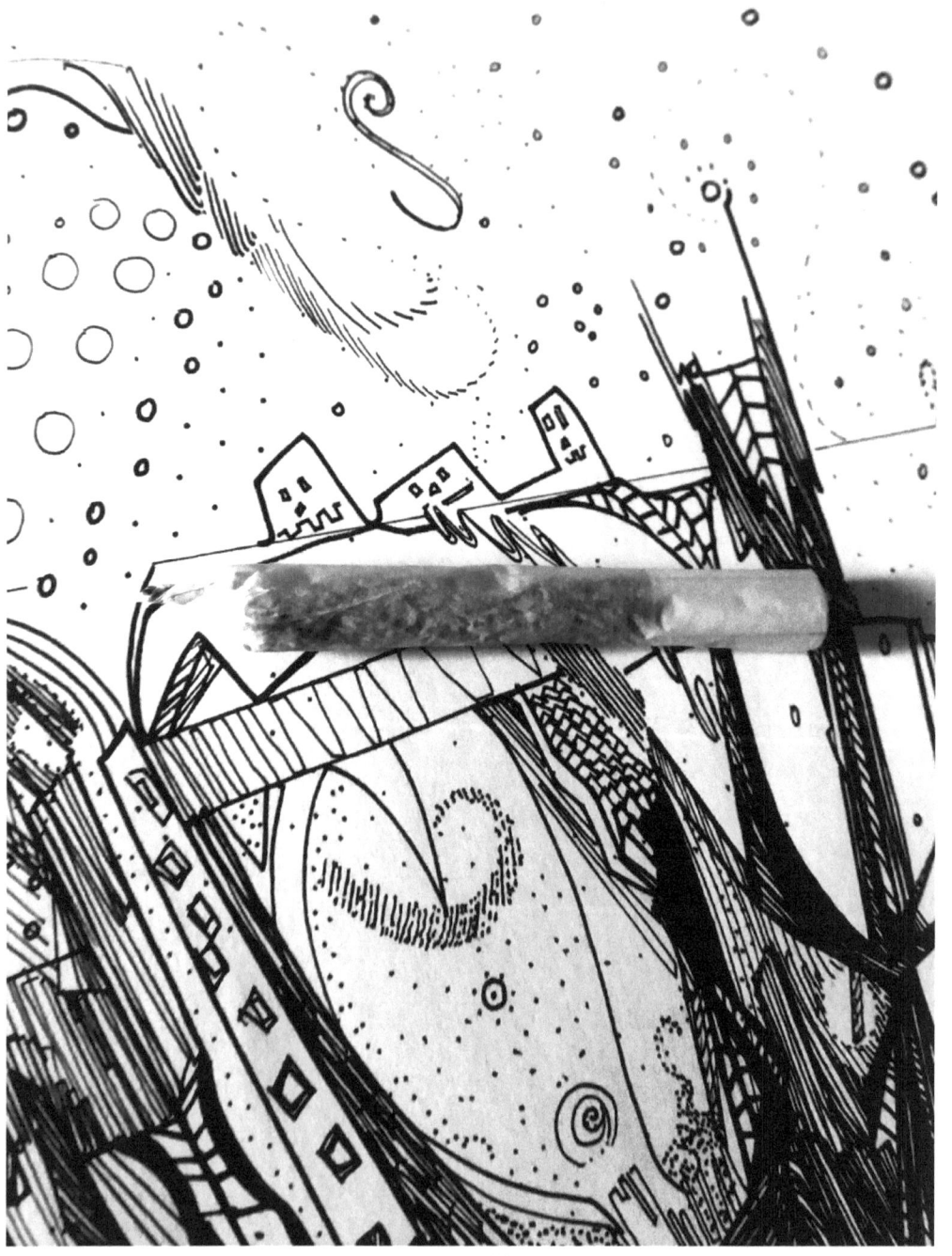

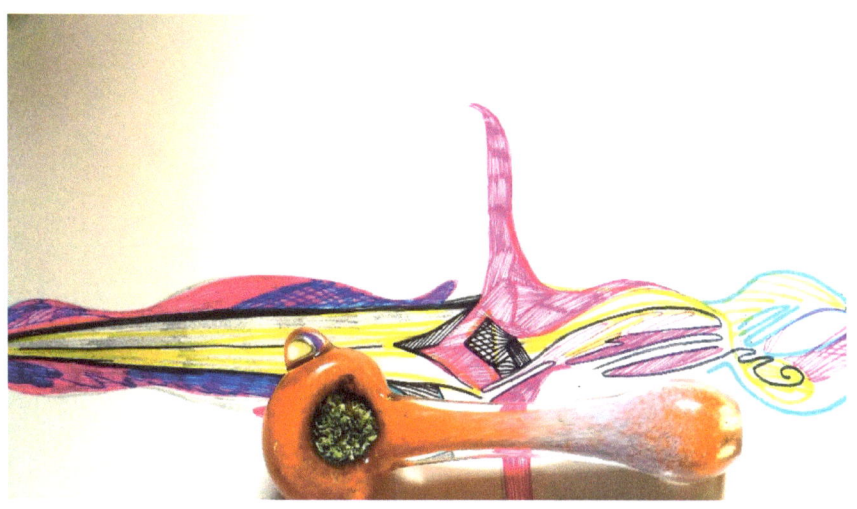

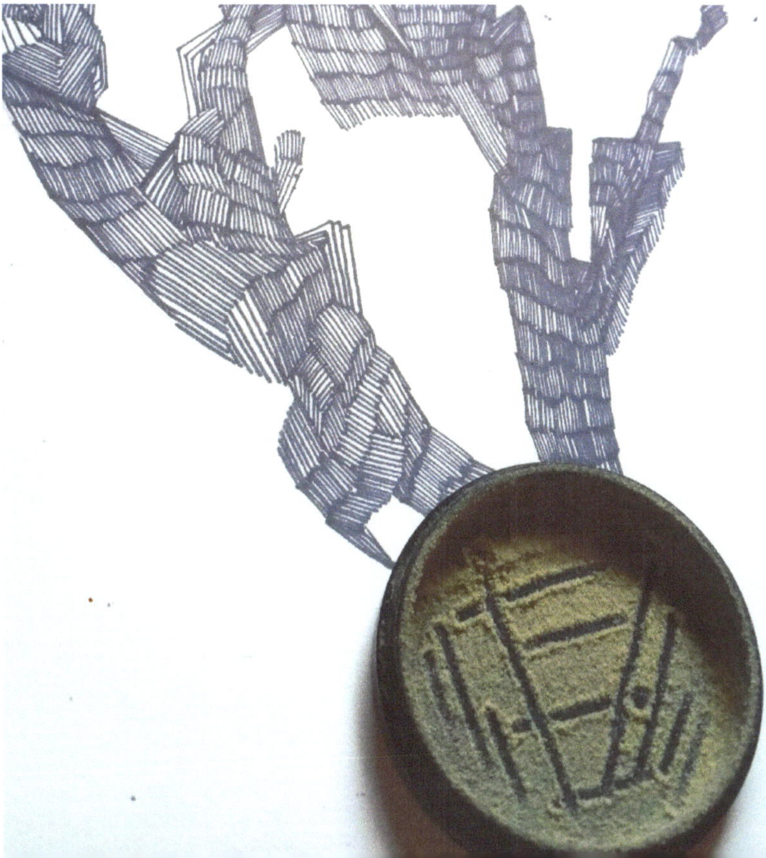

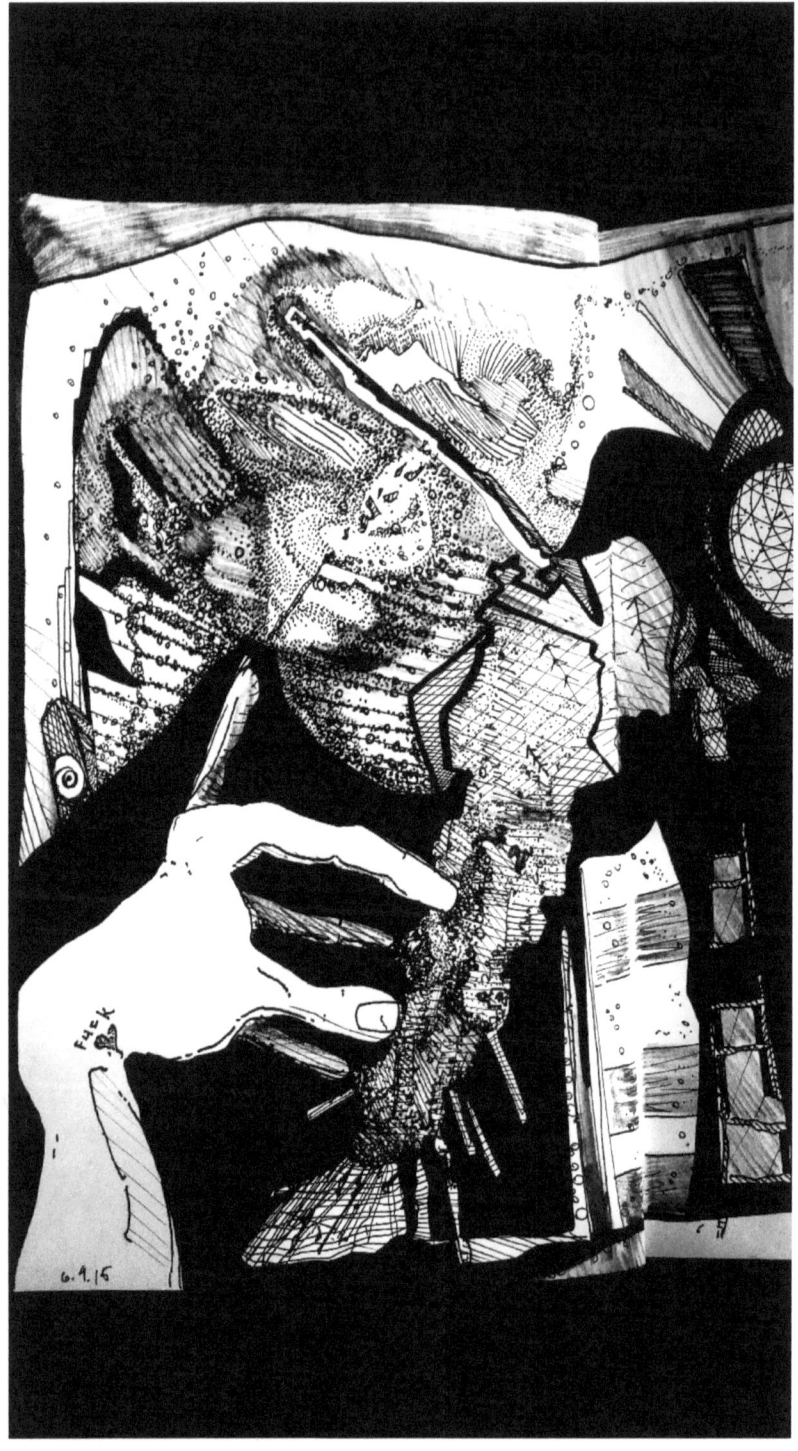

VACANT

I gutted my insides.

Anything soft and vulnerable was removed, carefully and tactfully. like a shady trauma surgeon, I performed emergency surgery on myself one winter. Ice cream scoops of feelings were excavated out of my being.

Two ice cold scoops of insecurities, a hot slice of self-pity, colorful sprinkles of jealousy.

The risks of the procedure didn't matter. I would not be my own worst enemy. My self-fed ego wouldn't allow it.

Survival depended on how effective my brain was functioning and

the way my heart was behaving...well, the foolish thing would have led me to suicide.

So, really,
logically,
anything mushy
had to go.

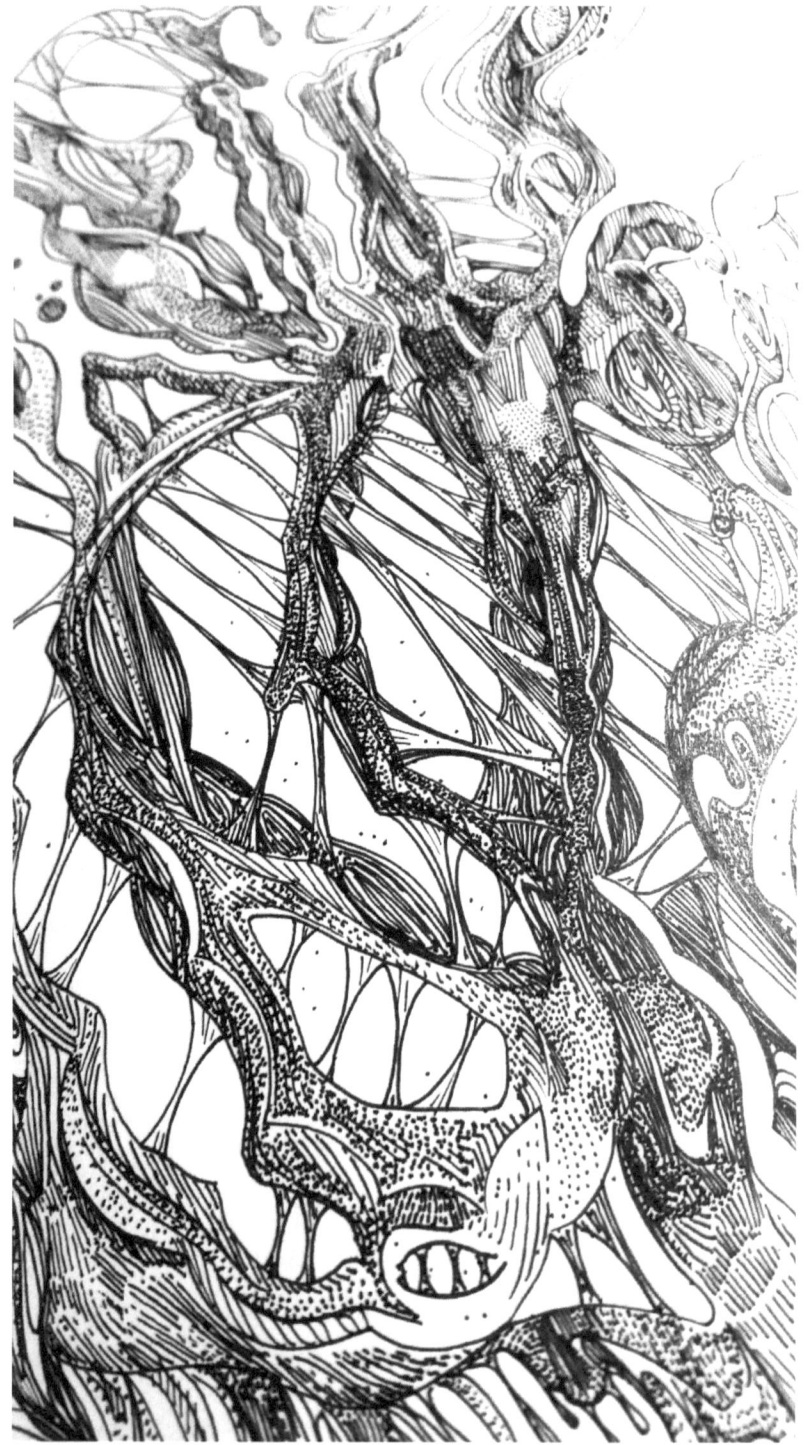

Pretty little thing, I wanna eat your life.
drink out all the innocent white.
Sell your body for a quarter tank of gas and let the world pass.
A pack of smokes,
A case of beer,
A few things,
to get out of here.
Its not personal, its financial.
I'll get mine because you got yours,
You got yours so I'll get mine.
pretty little thing,
don't waste your tears.
The course is set. So until then,
i'm out of here

park

She wants to
Kiss you
She wants to
Kill you
All at the
Same motherfucking
Time

Time

time plays tricks on the memory

But

Nothing beautiful demands attention

Don't let mixed signals fool you

Indecision is a decision

And says it all

The most annoying part is…
I'm not sure if she fooled me or if she's just fooling everyone else
Either way she's still a phony

I try to ignore her now
This display in front of me. The present fake.
And I try to preserve the memory of her I thought was real

That way,
I'm only fooling myself

An next time,
I'll know better

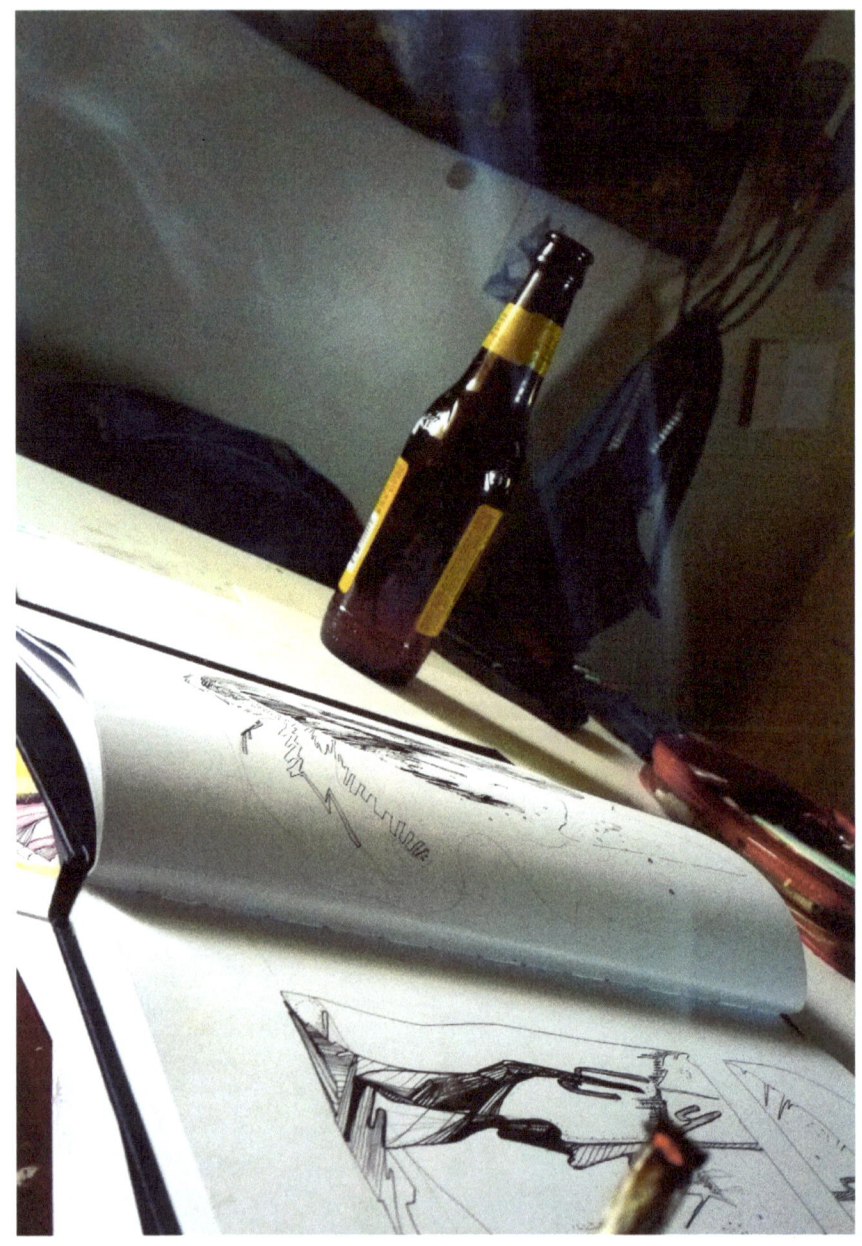

wRecked RePtiles

the quicker the sand the later the gator ambitious amphibians amplifying attitudes alphabetically starting with U, you.

chemically cracked kids question of the purpose of salty tears. looking unmotivated smelling underappreciated Asking themselves if ...you could love a little wiser?

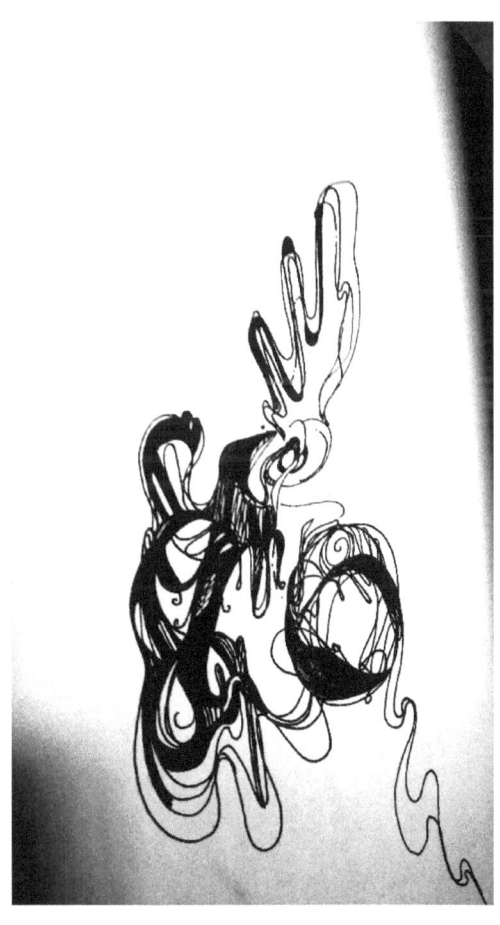

So now,

I got all these thoughts rolling around in my head
All these feelings in my belly
A nice big hole in my heart

And I wanna put some words down
To start
And
Well,
I
Got nothing

But time to spend
Overthinking and wondering
About all these other encounters
I let slip

To a lover or a friend

At least,

When I'm at work
I'm getting paid to sit around in the dark and contemplate
What the fuck I'm doing

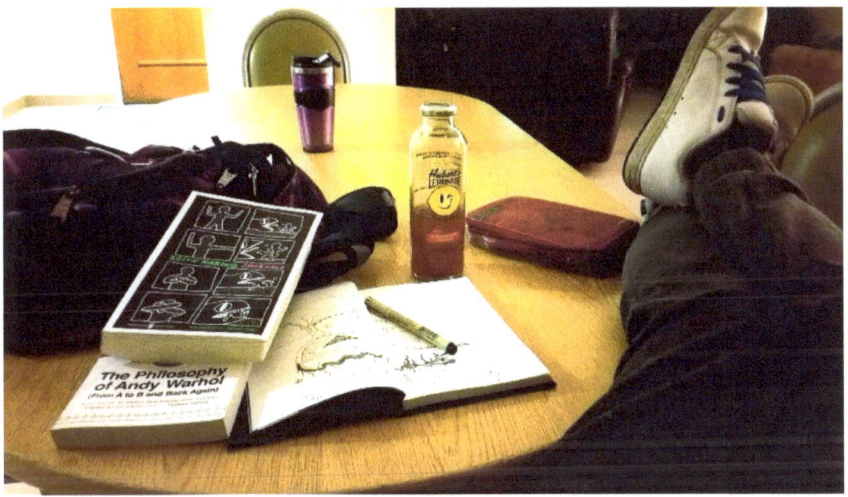

Every so often there are no words or cleaver quotes to neatly sum up the end of the day.
Sometimes you do everything right but it still feels like you've failed.

Either way
the day still ends.

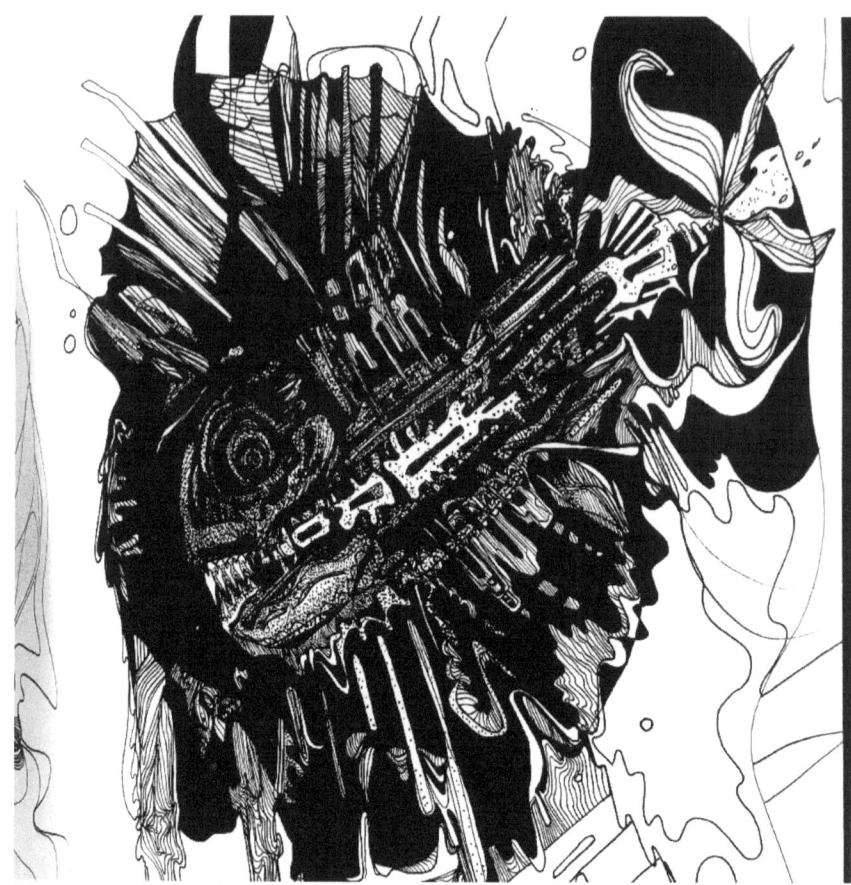

How long have I been walking around with shit on my shoe?
Soda stream my thoughts
    Bubbly carbonation
    It all supported my art habit
    Visions saturated on Saturdays
    That's how you know
    That's how you know the acid is working

She said, nothing says self-destruction like multiple wine hangovers. I said, nothing says sad slow self destruction like alcoholism

Paper cuts and stupidity acquired a strange group, an odd collection, of people too smart to be doing to what they were doing yet, too unmotivated to fix it. Uninspired. Separated by time and space, they weren't bad, just lost.

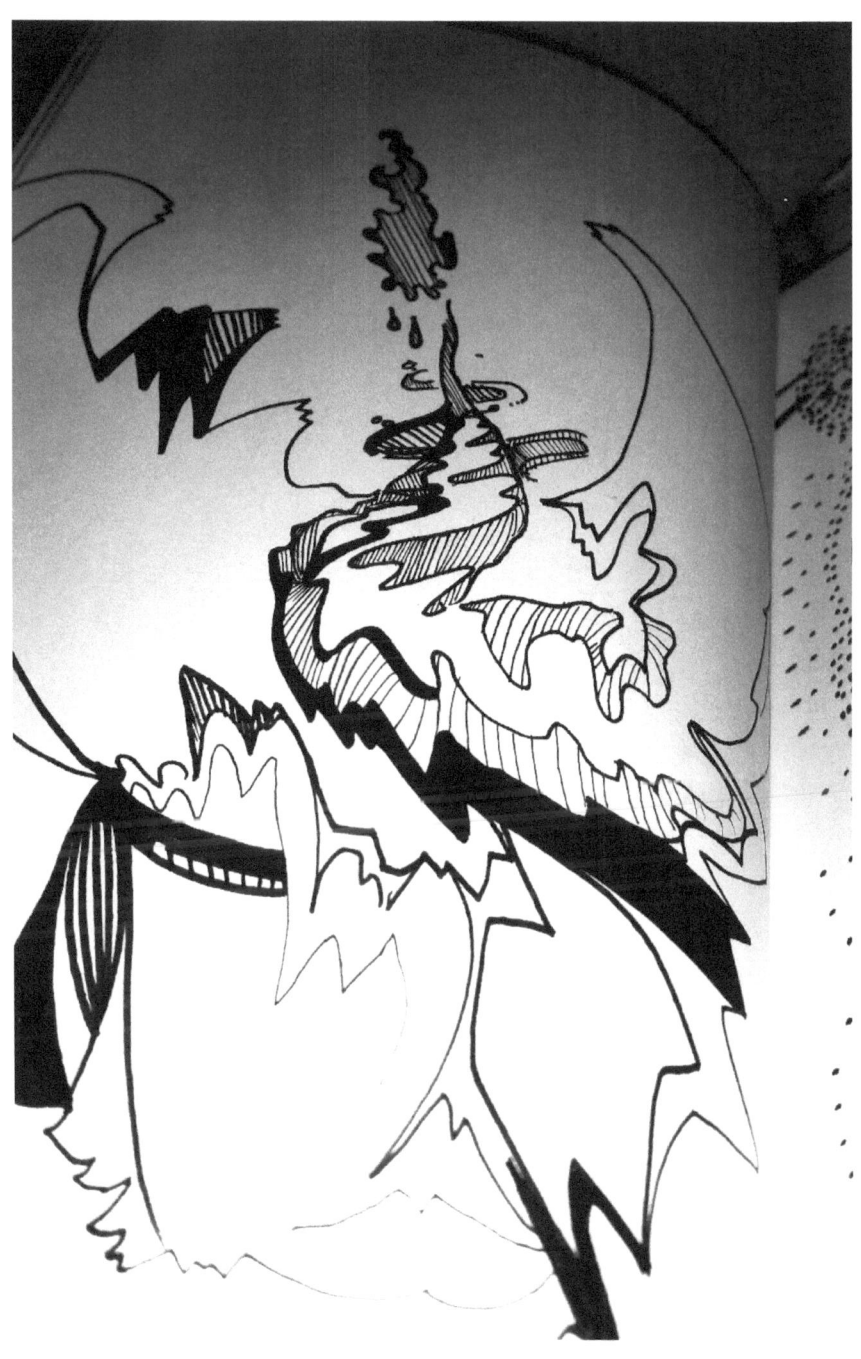

Oct 3 2014

Bright light burns my pupil and low light encourages imaginary
And the right chemical mixture
Makes me tipsy
And I lose
Myself in the forgotten familiar idea
Of sweetness
It blots my memory
And the bright light burns my pupils
An the low light comforts the lonely
And blotted memories make me tipsy
Lost in familiar imaginary

Hell: that really hot place that only plays country music

I've always been fairly observant, mostly when it comes to the environment (built or natural), not as so much when it comes to people. People are draining…people are not always true…their intentions not always pure…my passive aggressive curiosity is how I acquired my knowledge about the culture we are all born into. Forming thoughts inside my vessel of skin and bones I was building my perspective of the outside world. The habits, the traditions, the social norms and the societal hierarchy.

Later in life, I was regurgitating those thoughts and perspectives about the world I had experienced   in the form of art and simple poetry.

Later, later, in life I'd be releasing them into the world. This is my preferred method of purging. My salvation.

and it is self-serving. and possibly publicly beneficial.

We all have our demons.   If hell is endless eternal suffering, well, I've crafted my coping mechanism.

I've fine-tuned it like an American muscle car. kept it updated like a social media app.

It's not a weapon of violence, but a tool of communication. ammunition of thought.

it is sharp. And it is effective.

The power of propaganda.

The therapy of art.

j u s t   a   t h o u g h t .   .

park

You wake up on the
Floor of your room

Or
Your kitchen

of your house,

or
Apartment,
Or maybe its someone else's house
or apartment
Maybe you know them

Or maybe you dont

Whatever…

The irony is,
You pay rent at two locations
And sleep

at neither

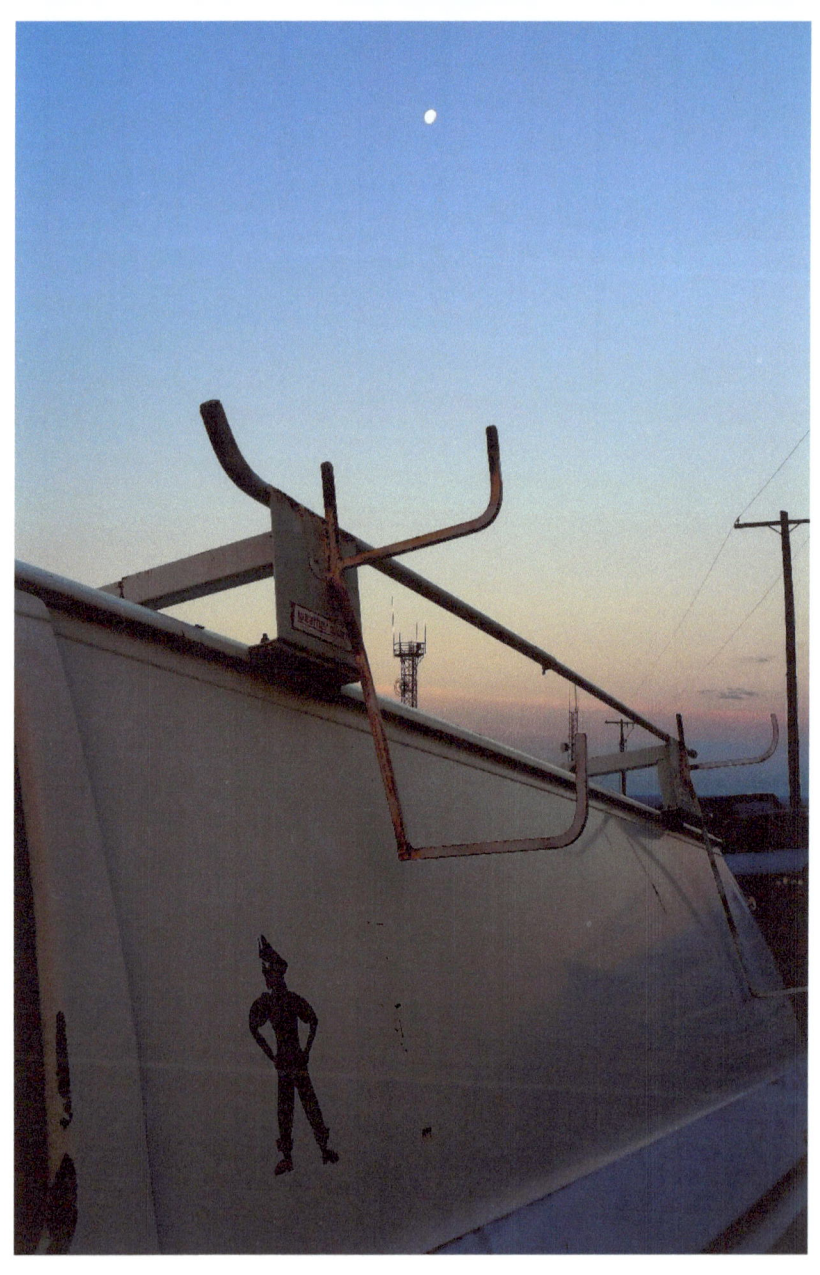

Eye stare

I stare

Mouth open and whisper

What the fuck is going on?

More often than not…

A lot practice method to the madness
Brains up in the attic that's attractive
Sorta seductive makes me panic
Fucking manic rusty outta shape romantic
Aaaahhh frantic
What's happening to me
My combative hat trick lost the advantage classically
charismatic got me
Caught me
playin with naughty nostalgic graphics
In my mind frame
Held against the wall
Posted notes penetrated
Thumbtacks dirty thoughts
Tickled when pinned with shame
but we still
Came
Hot and heavy
Secret so dirty
A lot practice
Method to the madness
Called when you're naked

She only calls

After last call

I only answer when I'm drunk

Glasses of glass
Crystal art containers
Holding sexy liquidity
Toxic yum nectar
High as hell
Cold as ice
Hmm(yeah)what?ever.

Even at late night
Even in the tacky diner light
Babe was bewitching
Clever cookie
crawling and craving
Delicious attitude teasing hands
Aggressively guiding you
Hunger in other forms
And fuck

You could just it lick up

Quiet howls hiding from the waiter
As he refills the cream in her hot coffee cup

park

Lapse in absurdity a stream of easy talk
Mortification exaggerated mystery
Kiss provoking lips
Sort stunned like easy prey
Eager and thirsty
unbelievingly hungry
Her world rose with subtle tones of pleasure
Smiling hills
Beyond the farthest edge into the dark inky night

Touch you
Cleanse me

of self interest
Covered in vegetation
wild vines of
Recreation
lightly grasping sheets of white

You want to regret nothing
Heavy breathing happiness torturing us
Drowsy drifting in visions
And dreams ecstasy endlessly shifting moods charging smiles
Expressing fine explosive chemistry
Everywhere

What a mess

I wanted to drain the false optimism from everyone
Let it bleed out all over the dirty tile floor
Puddle up beneath your designer shoes

Could we get any more foolish?
Could the young be any more naïve?

Happiness is cosmetic:
Purchase it at the mall
applied to surface in thick gooey layers

a quick-fix to the underlining mayhem

Keep applying, layer after layer,
Until everything is stained with beauty
Do not rinse, do not think
Repeat until everything becomes sticky
Until you can no longer smell the bullshit

We like it this way, full of pretty decoration
It helps us forget the evils
It helps us forget what we've done
How we aren't responsible,
How we have passed that point of no return
We are the cause of our collapse
We doomed
And when the world sets itself on fire
To rid itself of our self-destructive souls
We will cry and whimper,
Pretending not to understand
What we did to earn this fate

Fresh. Young. And foolish
there's so much more to this

She was born alone and she will die alone
Big lightning bolt to the heart

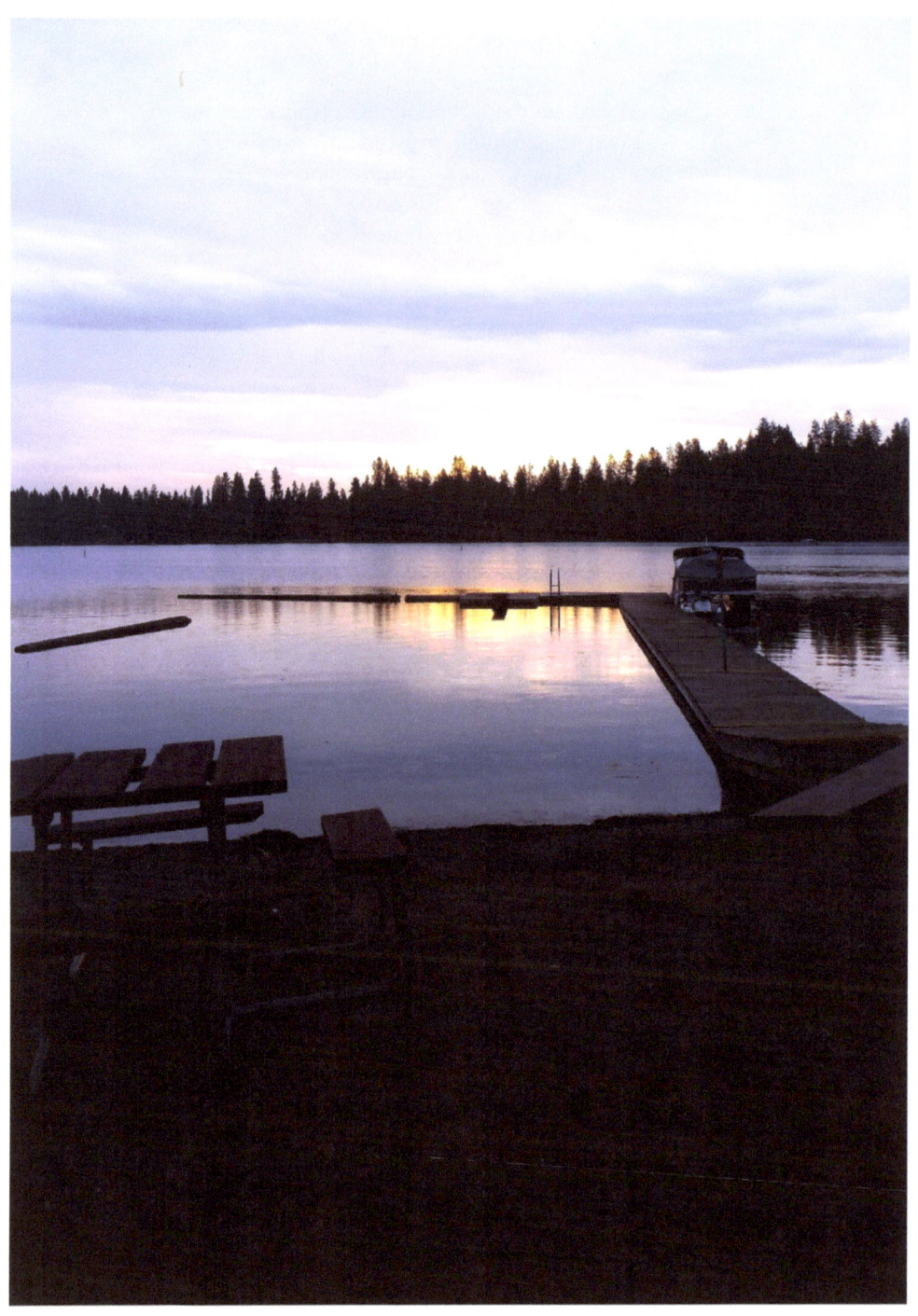

in case we get lost, damaged, or destroyed

i've been gone awhile.

sorry. This was a really great outlet for my thoughts and I've neglected
it.

I wish I had something special to share, you know?

a meaningful update about my life. Something insightful. But nothing
truly comes to mind,

I've been very stationary.

the older I get the less time I have to run away. I am definitely less self-
destructive than I once was. less reckless, less impulsive, less social.
I think my location and environment are major factors in this reclusive
behavior.

So, I've been keeping calm and drawing lines.
I am up all night trying to keep my mind occupied.
and it's difficult, I've lost my muse. communication died. I need a new
source.

another soul to jump start mine.
I haven't been searching and seeking, only dreaming.

Earlier today, i watching this tv show on the Netflix and one of the
character's said, "artists are doomed to a life of loneliness because they
cannot think beyond instant gratification" I must have replayed that part a
dozen times...

Anyways. In the fall, I'll be moving. hopefully I'll start painting.

again.
and writing a little more often.

park

One small town misfit
dreamer who dreams of quitting and drifting
a flustered painter
my mom says, you think I don't know you, you only think temporary
yea mom, I'm a disorganized child without a piggy bank

I like the dark, it hides the dirty
keep provoking, keep evolving
keep telling a story
keep thc
dope hope ….
the evergreen state
drip drip

park

9.1.2015

Instagram: park_art